All That Glitters

Plabita Bhaskar

Made with ❤ on the BookLeaf Publishing Platform
www.bookleafpub.in
www.bookleafpub.com

Dedication

To the universe who inspired me

to ink my thoughts into poetry.

Preface

This anthology is a collection of poems entwined with random emotions and life events of an ordinary girl. Poetry is all about feeling the emotions through verses. From the fragrance of a bud to song of a thrush, from seasons to weathers and sun, rain & sand. From falling in love to falling out of love; hook ups, patch ups, the rise and the falls; the highs and lows of life traverses. From relationships to people, from self doubt to self realization. This poetry book is a humble attempt to present life lessons in a poetic form. Hope you enjoy reading.

Love & warm hugs,
Plabita Bhaskar

Acknowledgements

This book is a piece of my heart, dedicated to my mother first for gifting me with the art of scribbling sweet prose and poetry. My dearest husband for his endless love and support. My dear siblings for being my constant cheerleader and my little Baby Debarya for being the love, light and sunshine of my life.

1. The Highland Lass

An oriental lass,
Petite stature, nimble feet
Deep ebony placid eyes
Pearl white dentures, voice so sweet.

Tresses as black as the long dark night
Round plush cheeks
Rounded hips.
She walks like a breeze
Her perfumed whiff.
She sways like branches of a cherry blossom tree.

She beckons spring with her carefree laughs
Jingle monsoon with every graceful spin
In her beautiful heart she carries mammoth love.
A warm summer brook, an affectionate stream.

She dances with the moon and slide through the tides.
She's a beacon of love, of warmth, of light.
A canopy of stars sprouting through her veil

She's fearless, she's a valiant knight.

Untamed, unbound, seamless soul
Ignorant of rage, of steaming foul.
Men O' Men, those that are poor gentry
You carping cliques, predatory kin.

Your cold snares and stooping dejection
Mindless babbles and hideous intentions.
Stop choking the carefree soul.
Let the thrush sing the sweetest song
Together you tune in unison.
Hail and embrace the rising sun.
Let love and only love soothe the
Ageless agony.
Let her be the way she is
Let her rewrite her own beginning.

****

2. They will say

They will talk, whatsoever it is
They think they must and would never fail.
Adjudge, oppress.
Force to dwindle your faith
Keep you from the good and try to slay.
Some words would be wise and lit your mind.
Some to demean and push you hind.
Be smart and righteous,
Witty and sage.
Pick from the ocean of blues
The pebbles that mark your way.

****

3. The Spectators of Eve Tease

Do you care to haste or to act
Except just to see
When you are there, just as me and you see
He's feasting in his mind
About my body, as he stands there and stares at me.
Devouring me in his fancied hideous mind
He licks and he bites his lips in fantasy,
His words cut through my dress
My torso, my skin;
When his eyes damn!!
As he stares at me.

Despaired, discomforted my untouched plight
I frantically look around for a safe haven.
Our eyes met twice
I could see that you are seeing
But you chose to look away!!
Perhaps you are that man who is used to it.
Perhaps you are somebody who loves this play.
My body, his treat.
You are still looking, but you walk away...

Now I'm sure of this and I know

You love it this way.
Sadly, you are that somebody who is used to it
And you love this play.

Isn't it Daunting!!
Don't you feel sick??? She's out in the wilderness
Happy and free.
Your sister, your friend,
Your mother, your aunt.
Those eyes still there
Always hunting.
Cold and staring.
You ought to know this
These morons you ignore are at ease
As you please.

Don't you care, don't you think??
You are at guilt as you walk away...
Cause you choose to be dumb.
Lest a word, just numb.
Or is it really true
Like I think you to be.
That perhaps you are that man who is used to it.
Perhaps you are somebody who loves this play.
Perhaps this, perhaps that...
Perhaps.... (Sigh!!)

****

4. The Middle Child

I was never a Daddy's Princess
Nor do I remember when I was cradled to sleep.
A middle child was left with the Granny to raise
Mumma Papa there, yet a mile away...
Just like the game of hide and seek.

Middle child! Middle child!
Oh! She's a little dunce you see.
Middle child! Middle child!
She's hostile, she breaks free...

Uncradled, uncuddled
She quests for mini gifts
Untamed, unrest.
She fusses, she gets into tiffs.

She would make room for the siblings dear
Make errands and fix small odds.
Hawk eyed; Bulls eye she would hit.
Her dreams big and shrewd mind, not dimwit.

No mount of dolor could tear her soul
She's a warrior, she conquers
A supernova unbound.
She's your middle child you least cared.
She's a loner, she's the hound.

****

5. Bulletproof

If your skin didn't grow thicker yet
Mark these words dear kith and kin.
Words will cut, words will balm
Words cause pain, words that glum.
Act no more, be bulletproof.
Think no more, be bulletproof.

They ought to say things; now and forever
Things that would haunt
Words that kill. Words to taunt.
Oh, dear you so fat!! Oh, sigh she's too thin.
Dark skin, tanned skin, scars and marks.
Small eyes, big nose, like ghouls their barks.
Your salary, your closet, your credit cards, your phone.
Your house, your car, your belongings, your loan.
Mindless blabbers, endless talks...
Words that suffer, words that haunt.
The Pseudo critics, the Pap talk aunts
Condemn, denounce, deject, deceive
Belittle, adjudge, prosecute, aggrieve.

Don't succumb my friend
Hark not the vice
Deafen them with your triumphant victory
Hear no more, be soundproof.
Act no more, be bulletproof.
Think no more, be bulletproof.

****

6. Mirrors

A crystalline plane
Reflecting a twin figure of me
Complacent its incandescent beam.
I fooled the world in camouflage,
The Mirrors revealed my whim.

The scales of truth, hard undefined.
Masquerading world in tales of lies,
The fear of defeat was ever beneath,
Invincible masks to veil my vulnerability.

Oh! but the pristine crystalline plane,
Its spying light and a helpless me.
The veil of disguise so melted through,
For the mirrors can't contort
My daunting fears, my voiceless screams.

****

7. Mother

You gleam bright in mild fluorescence.
Like a soothing sun, on a wintry day.
Amidst the hordes of people dense,
Your face a rare fond countenance.

A glimpse of you is paradise,
I bow my head in reverence.
Juxtapose to God's abode,
Is your idol clad in your sentience.

Hymns so soft, you would gently hum,
Salve my dreary soul.
From miles your vocal, tears my heart,
A restive child, I lose my calm.

From a toddler to adolescence
In your love clad arms I grow,
So long far miles I perambulate,
Home is predestined.

So hard life's traverse defile me,
Mum, home is where I shall come.

13

****

8. Soul Redemption

Burning like the incense sticks
My sanctity mere a wisp of smoke.
The flame swallows me low and slow,
Draping me to the pit of my soul.

My ashes heap, my corpse lay low.
The cologne mixed in air.
If burning be my redemption,
My Lord!! So be it so.

****

9. Lovers

Your smile a mystic flamboyance
Like a moonlit night profound.
A cozy heart that cajoles me,
Like a lyrical hallowed psalm.

Your sweat like misty redolence,
Touch of velvet skin.
A torso built like Hercules,
Lips like saccharine.

Your rhythmic waggish salsa moves,
Catalyze adrenaline waves.
Songs you sing to cradle me,
Way, you lock in warm embrace.
The cosmos witness's epic tales,
The nimbus rain love grains.
Our secret tryst is secured deep,
In the heavens safe from pains.
****

10. Dear Rain

Get drenched fall free nimbus dear,
Cleanse the dreary soul.
The wind sings tales of agony,
Take a fancy stroll.

Fill your misty redolence,
Jingle the crystalline beads.
Pick your groovy love crayon,
Brush your rainbow shades upon.

The frolic puddle to hop around
Paper boats to sail.
Earthy sandy petrichor
Splay some magic, love profound.

****

11. Out of Love

Has time hackneyed your love my dear!
Or is it just an awful day??
Has petals of love withered away,
Was the sun too hot today??

So do we choose to live or stay without
Are we cozy being apart??
Should I blame my stars and the constellation above??
Should I drench in pain, my heart??

Would you cup my chin and brush your breathe
Or push me to the blues.
Would you gently spin me in the air,
Or scavenge our love hues??

My heart chokes hard,
I struggle to breathe
I'm a human and not a thing.
Must you say what shenanigan
You play to hurt a being.

Is it just another fateful day
and the dusk would never near.
With winter fall, the spring come close

and life would ever be dear.

****

12. Tears

Trickle down slow,
No hustle, no race,
Drop down till you evanesce.

Wet soul, clasped hold,
Aching hour.
Dank wind, hate pins,
Hurt no more.

Raucous wailing,
Flustered soul,
Grave numb sobbing,
In voiceless bawl.

Drip down flow,
Oh! tears break slow.
Drop down till you fall no more.

****

13. Sleep Bonita!

Why can't you sleep, Oh dear! poor soul.
The time wafts by, sings the dreary owl.
You saw the nightfall under the sky;
The moonlit night stood still
You cried!!
The moisten cheeks so pallid now
and lips dried out, so dearth of sleep.

What mount of dolor heaps in your heart??
That chokes so hard, as you struggle to sleep.
What tales of lie you meekly unfold!
Why do you veil your thoughts untold?
When God of Love brace you in charm
Where do you hide your pain sublime?
Your tryst with him is hallowed you say,
Why then is your plight arcane?

The spring did come
The love birds' tweet,
You said it trickled like a bad blood stream.
The blossoms dried in a mournful sight,

The cuckoo sang a dirge polite.
Then from dusk to dawn, from daylight to night
You stared in a motionless still.
The scorching sun bathed the pains
The tumultuous storm, washed your dusty lane.
Still, you weep, in voiceless bawl.
Your tears testament the night profound.
Your weary eyes still beautiful,
Your ears that longed a soothing verse.

Sleep Bonita!
You wept all night.
and sleep must come to thee.
The morbid days are here for a while
See how the Sun cajoles you with a smile.
Sleep while the rainbow leaps upon and
Love birds sing a lullaby.
Sleep dear one, for you must sleep!
and sleep must come to thee.

****

14. Sacrosanct Love?

If love is ever sacrosanct
The sky won't fall
The earth won't bleed
No turbulent tempest blow.
No trace of ego vehement,
Would play a game of foul.
Nor rancor blues of hatred hurt.
Scavenge bonds of gold.
No cutthroat words slay love bird's dear
Would a demon feed of them???
Would poles of trust be crushed upon,
If love is sacrosanct.

****

15. Life after death

When death drew near
and I felt it breathing under my neck.
My spine forbade chilling
Nor did my blood clot cold
My eyes were still warm.
I embraced every inch of the dreadful death hug.
Warming threads of its silky black gown.
Slowly and steadily we melted through.
Wisped into smoke of eternity...

What is lies beyond death??
When curtains hung low and lights turn off.
Where does the soul go??
Well I flew against the gravity.
I swam across the deepest shore.
In death and beyond is serenity
and I live, yes I live!!
Living more than when I was living.
Breathing through the infinity of spaces.
Between time and reality.
I heard the ruffling sound
As my wings untied and fluttered.
I could then fly.
Soaring to the zenith of enlightenment.

Fly like I never would.
Fly cause I then couldn't.
I whispered a word
and the nimbus roared.
Pushed a cloud to break free.
It's been raining for hours and
My soul is soaked and drenched.
Wet in the goodness of unliving tears.
I cried, cried tears of joy.
I am not a prisoner.
Not anymore!
I am unbound and I soar and I'm flying.
Dead still living.
I didn't die, I live through my death.
Lest dreadful, death brought me alive!!

****

16. I was watching you

When you were sitting alone,
Your mind unrest.
Lines strewn hard on thy forehead.
Crystalline droplets your eyes that shed,
Together in sync my heart did bled.
I know you trembled, you feared, despaired.
You weren't alone,
For I was there, watching you.

Yours palms so clasped with pray full tears,
That rack you ensembled your pain in layers.
Those grave heavy breathe you helplessly sighed!
That smile you would wear to discreetly hide.
I know you trembled, you feared, despaired.
You weren't alone.
I was still there, watching you.

How in agony you silently bawled
That pints of happiness you toiled to fall.
Your voiceless screams,
Every crushed dream.

When you lowered your head and drenched in pain.
You weren't alone Mum
Strangled to defeat.
My heart was trembling too.
I know your soul, your dreams behold.
You weren't ached alone.
For I was always there watching you.

****

17. Childhood

My mind a mini parachute,
It takes a fancy spin.
Fly me miles in the misty air,
As I gossip with the wind.

I gently perch on a groovy pine,
From the heights I look behind.
A tint of light, peeps with a smile
Like a speck from the past time.

A lane so rosy, vivid memoirs,
I feel my pulse breakthrough
I chance to glimpse my childhood days,
In the dungeon I walk through.

Giggles and whispers and wishful smiles
Eyes that spark new dreams.
My siblings lovely like the sun,
Their love a holy stream.

The toddler tunes I struggled to sing
The toys molded of clay.
My bath tub a tiny pristine bay,
My cotton couch to lay.

I smell the silky jaggery brown,
In the misty air above.
Chimes of childhood echoes still.
Play my gloomy town.

****

18. Verses Pal

Like a beam, it rinses through,
My heart was never opaque.
So, I heed a gentle persuasive nod
and allow the words to sing.

Sing a song, oh! words thy vocal;
Smears like a poesy balm.
Pat and cradle,
Soothe and fondle,
How gentle feels your palm.

A Brooke of words that flows profound,
Words submerge me within.
Fish me out from a dank tunnel,
Words my kith, my kin.

****

19. Who needs to be heard

Hours creep crawling, leisurely.
A second a year it seems.
I fix my eyes to the ceiling above.
The concrete can hear my screams.

I have heard them do it.
Commit it and succumb to it!!
Hanging choking and fighting to peace
And they do it with much chivalry.
Thousands of mouths recklessly taunt
A coward, a loser a naysayer perhaps.
I listen to them all silently though
Inside I can feel their pain.

Borderline syndrome, depressed, oppressed
Addict, schizophrenic and sick.
Easy to conclude, easier to verdict.
One who breathes the living pain would know

How masquerading pain with a joyful smile feels.
What an ail it is to laugh through pains
And walk home broken with tears and rains.

Hug them, love them,
Take them out.
Life is beautiful, embrace the odds.
Love is the elixir, consume the happy pods.
Let not darkness doom your day
Do not succumb dear friend.
With the giant waves rise up and find your way.

****

20. The Lethargy

My days are all so indolent.
As I stroll across the corridor,
My eyes fixed at the huge round clock.
I binge and I lull so deep.

The intermittent cacophony hits the wall of my ears,
My neurons reacts the least.
My eye lids twine the waterline beneath
As I murmur, let me sleep.

I rise like a mammoth, still half asleep
My den a mountain of debris.
Attire that was worn out and left
Accessories so paired and forsaken.
The snickers, the ballerinas, the satchels around
All jaded and left forgotten.

I dragged my torso in baby steps ahead,
snoozed the alarm for the fifth in a row.
My throat so dry, as I lift the empty bottle
and off to my bed I surrender again.

Popped out an eye from the quilt, as I peep
The nimbus clamor and rains
The air around breaks a lullaby,
I'm lethargic, oh!! let me sleep.

****

21. The Last Message

Tell my solitary
Silence is golden.
Tell my integrity,
Faith is immortal.

Whisper my strengths,
Weakness is a challenge.
Whisper my griefs,
Hope is sunshine.

Ask my dreams,
If they fear to shatter?
Tell my mind
Courage is invincible.

Whisper my corpse
No soul demise
Time is sorcery
Life is but sly.

Convey my love,
To my foes and my kin.
I aced the life race,
Death crowns my win.

****